Me and My Friends

I Can Listen

written by Daniel Nunn

illustrated by Clare Elsom

Chicago, Illinois

© 2015 Heinemann Library,
an imprint of Capstone Global Library, LLC
Chicago, Illinois

All rights reserved. No part of this publication may be reproduced or transmitted in any form or by any means, electronic or mechanical, including photocopying, recording, taping, or any information storage and retrieval system, without permission in writing from the publisher.

Edited by Brynn Baker
Designed by Steve Mead and Kyle Grenz
Production by Helen McCreath
Original illustrations © Clare Elsom
Originated by Capstone Global Library Ltd

Library of Congress Cataloging-in-Publication Data
Cataloging-in-publication information is on file with the Library of Congress.

ISBN 978-1-4846-0246-1 (paperback)
ISBN 978-1-4846-0256-0 (ebook PDF)

Contents

Listening 4
Listening Quiz 20
Picture Glossary 22
Index 22
Notes for Teachers
and Parents 23
In this Book. 24

Listening

I **listen** to my **friend**.

My friend listens to me.

I listen to my mom.

My mom listens to me.

I listen to my brother.

My brother listens to me.

I listen to my sister.

My sister listens to me.

I listen to my dad.

My dad listens to me.

I listen to my teacher.

My teacher listens to me.

I listen to our dog.

Our dog listens to me.

I listen to everyone!

Everyone listens to me!

Listening Quiz

Which of these pictures shows listening?

Did listening make this child happy? Why? Do you listen?

Picture Glossary

friend person you care about and have fun with

listen to hear with your ears, paying close attention to the purpose of the words

Index

brothers 8, 9
dads 12, 13
dogs 16, 17
friends 4, 5

moms 6, 7
sisters 10, 11
teachers 14, 15

Notes for Teachers and Parents

BEFORE READING

Building background: Ask children to whom they listen during the school day. (friends, teachers, bus drivers) To whom do they talk when they get home? (family members)

AFTER READING

Recall and reflection: Have children look at page 13. Ask them what the girl and her dad talked about. Have children look at page 9. Ask what the brothers talked about.

Sentence knowledge: Ask children to find a capital letter and a period in the book. Why is there a capital letter? Why is there a period?

Word knowledge (phonics): Have children point to the word *dad* on page 12. Sound out the three phonemes in the word *d/a/d*. Ask children to sound out each phoneme as they point at the letters, and then blend the sounds together to make the word *dad*. Have children name some words that rhyme with *dad*. (glad, sad, mad, bad)

Word recognition: Have children count how many times the word *listen/listens* appears in the main text (not counting the quiz). (16)

AFTER-READING ACTIVITIES

Have children work with partners to listen and speak. As one child tells about a topic, such as what he or she did over the weekend, the other should listen and then name two things he or she remembers from listening. Then the partners should switch roles.

In this Book

Topic
listening

Topic Words
brother
dad
everyone
friend
listen
mom
sister
teacher

Sentence Stems
I ___ to my mom.
Our ___ ___ to me.
I ___ to my ___.
My ___ listens to ___.

High-frequency Words
I
our
me
my
to